THE MINDSTRETCH

49 INSPIRING INSIGHTS FOR BUSINESS BREAKTHROUGHS

Barry Laub | Dean Mercado

New York, USA

Limit of Liability/Disclaimer of Warranty

To our loving and supporting family members...
You are the reason why!

And a thank you to those who have worked with us and
revealed to us what was needed in this book!

CONTENTS

PREFACE

$\mathcal{F}$rom our very first conversation together, we knew we were destined to work together. Although separated in age by two decades, we resonated on a deeper level than either of us had experienced before with others professionally... besides our wives of course! ☺

Over the years, each of us having worked with entrepreneurs and business professionals has observed the gaps which impede success... pieces of the puzzle were missing. This book that you are reading begins filling those gaps... providing some of those missing pieces so to speak. It is not intended to be an all encompassing dissertation for the disciplines it covers.

In case you were wondering, one of the reasons we wrote this book (besides the fact that we both felt we were long overdue to write one) was to have fun. We both have an insatiable desire for wisdom, self growth...

and sharing. Yes, we consider these things fun!

In creating this book, we kept our commitment to meet at least twice per week. These sessions were *INTENSE!* Yet they had plenty of room for playfulness. Our success was accomplished by transcending ego. There was no competition... just sincere mutual admiration.

We often commented that we should have recorded every session... in hindsight we were right... oh well, lesson learned.

This truly was a work of love. We hope that you gain as much from the insights as we did in coming up with them.

Barry and Dean

INTRODUCTION

*W*hat are you holding in your hand? Is it a book? Is it a manual? Is it a source guide for coaches? Is it a human behavior amplifier? Is it a workshop? Is it a mastermind topic opener?

The answer is *YES* to all and more!

In this book we explore 7 essential disciplines for businesses (Envision, Believe, Plan, Lead, Communicate, Market, and Sell) providing 7 insights for each. The intent is to take you deep... expanding the confines of traditional thinking... into a state of awareness which we call "The Mindstretch".

Every word in this book has been carefully crafted and selected for optimal impact and clarity. We literally discussed each one down to the level of... "should the word here be 'of' or 'for' and how does each change the meaning of the insight?" While it may sound a bit over the top, we strongly believe that the energy that language delivers is powerful and its proper use improves results exponentially.

Although this book is not intended to be read cover to cover in one fell swoop as you would a novel, we do recommend reading at least one entire discipline at a time and then going back and selecting which insight you would like to focus on first.

In the epilogue, we provide a system called the "Power of SEVEN". It is intended to act as a stimulus for you to draw the most value out of each insight. In a nutshell, SEVEN is an acronym for...

- ☯ Stretch *your mind...*
- ☯ Establish *objective...*
- ☯ Visualize *results...*
- ☯ Empower *manifestation...*
- ☯ Nurture *growth...*

We suggest that you contemplate the insights, reread them, meditate on them, journal your thoughts, or simply just "be" with them and see what shows up for you. There is no right or wrong way to benefit from them.

This book is intended to help you focus on purpose and objective. If you keep this in mind throughout, you will gain many treasures as they unfold. It is a way of cleansing and intending in order to manifest what you desire.

Although you can certainly work on these insights alone, we do recommend working on them with a mastermind or a coach who is not attached to you experiencing a specific outcome. This approach will further expand what is possible for you.

Make this book come alive for you. It is meant to be an evolving stimulator. While the disciplines are designed for business enhancement, each insight will apply to some aspect of your business and personal life. It is up to you to connect the dots. Just as with poetry, interpretations are personal and limitless.

Business and life are much more rewarding and fun when you play full out... enjoy the journey!

What we tell ourselves is our truth and truth is nothing more than a belief. Our beliefs are driven by our subconscious programming. Our subconscious programming is the culmination of our life's experiences... our successes... our failures... and how others addressed, and we translated those experiences.

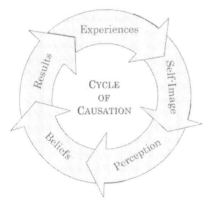

All of this can be summed up in a paradigm which we call the *"Cycle of Causation"*.

EXPERIENCES **influence** **your** **SELF-IMAGE...**

Every moment of life is a learning experience... Your interpretation of that experience influences your degree of fear or level of confidence...

we call that the "self-image continuum".

SELF-IMAGE influences your PERCEPTION...
The self-image continuum spans from fear to confidence. Your position on that continuum colors how you see yourself and your expectations.

PERCEPTION influences your BELIEFS...
Perception is greater than reality... there is no such thing as one finite reality... only one's perception.

BELIEFS influence your RESULTS...
The universe responds to the vibrational energy of what you believe. This manifests into result.

RESULTS in turn, influence your EXPERIENCES...

Thus the cycle continues.

STAY FOCUSED...
and allow yourself to
SEE BIG!

You Are The

Creator...

The choices are yours!

❧ You can choose to accept, mitigate, or eliminate whatever you conceive. Accept your responsibility!

❧ Owning your choice(s) and standing by them demonstrates your strength of character!

❧ Tackle tough decisions. Look within. Get clear on what you want!

insight 2

Yes

You Can...

Be Unstoppable!

❂ Allow possibilities to emerge. Embrace their potentiality!

❂ Seize the opening. Push through the fear. Allow manifestation!

❂ Risk is the mother of greatness. Go for it!

Understand Your
Programming...
The present does not have to mimic your past!

 ☯ Examine your current reality. Identify what is working and what is not!

 ☯ Identify and acknowledge anything that may be impeding you!

 ☯ Stay focused on your "why". Move ahead!

insight 4

Money is
Infinite...
Energize its flow!

- ☯ Your belief that you deserve abundance activates its flow!

- ☯ Giving purposefully without strings attached activates its flow!

- ☯ Coming from a space of gratitude activates its flow!

Believing Is

Seeing...

Use faith as your guide!

- A key to manifesting is in knowing what you want and believing you deserve it!

- Once you believe, do not allow anything to dissuade you... be unwavering!

- Your belief opens the doorway to boundless manifestation!

Be True To Your
Instincts...
Trust and engage!

- ☯ Instincts are pure. They will lead you to your vision!

- ☯ Fuel your subconscious with positivity. Improve your instincts!

- ☯ Your results are dependent upon your level of self-confidence!

Seek

Social Proof...

Validation is inspiration!

- ☯ The human condition by nature requires and thrives on validation!

- ☯ Create an environment that provides the reinforcement needed to drive you further!

- ☯ If you desire social proof, deliver it!

DISCIPLINE 2

ENVISION!

KNOW WHY YOU WANT
WHAT YOU WANT

*S*uccessful entrepreneurs have vision! They have vision driven by a strong and passionate "why", a "why" that awakens them with the burning desire to make it happen, a "why" that continuously propels them toward that vision and because they love what they are creating, a "why" that makes it difficult to shut down at the end of the day.

Creating and running a business without a clearly defined vision is akin to setting sail on the ocean without much thought as to where you want to go. Oh you will get somewhere; however that somewhere will likely lead you astray as the ocean in its vastness has its way with you!

The key difference... is operating from a space of proaction, as opposed to reaction. You will be happier and more successful as the one who creates, rather than the created!

Implementing a vision is not for the meek. Naysayers will criticize and roadblocks may occur... that is just par for the course. Seeing beyond those distractions is made possible by a strong and clear "why".

Additionally, a vision without the courage to implement is just a pipedream... a pattern of unrealized pipedreams can be deflating for the entrepreneur, causing them to think small and shun risk, branding them subconsciously (and consciously) as just a dreamer, not a doer... ultimately setting them up to fail... this is not a good space for the entrepreneur to operate from.

STAY FOCUSED...
and allow yourself to
SEE BIG!

insight 8

Uncover Your

Passion...

Be ignited every day!

☯ A business driven by passion is magnetic and magnetic businesses foster advancement!

☯ Clearly communicated passion generates enthusiasm and it is that enthusiasm that people find contagious! Those contagions create a viral effect for business!

☯ Caution, passion will ebb and flow. It requires ongoing kindling to keep it ablaze!

insight 9

Own Your
"WHY"...
Be completely committed!

- Your passion *is* your "why". Your "why" is what drives you in fulfilling your objective.

- Others will pick up on your level of commitment to your "why" and act in kind!

- A committed "why" magnetizes you and your business thus attracting those who want what you have to offer.

Possibilities are

Boundless...

Every new idea is crazy until it works!

- ❧ Think small, receive small... think big, receive big. Business excellence requires operating from a place of abundance!

- ❧ Your true limitations are those that are self-imposed!

- ❧ Critics will always be there to challenge your unorthodox ideas! Consenting to critics hinders innovation!

insight 11

Palm Tree
Tenacity...
Bend without breaking!

- ☯ Your business will experience turbulence. Have the fortitude to be unstoppable!

- ☯ Build your business firmly rooted in your "why". This reinforces your staying power!

- ☯ Adversity brings opportunity... breakdowns lead to breakthroughs!

Formulate Your
Pathway...
Begin with the objective in mind!

- Be crystal clear on where you want to be (i.e. destination) and where you actually are now (i.e. source).

- Lay out the stepping stones needed to get you where you want be. These take on the form of measurable goals!

- Embrace the inspiration of others. However, your ideal path is unique to you!

insight 13

Change is

Inevitable...

Embrace it!

☯ Fear of change stifles growth. Acceptance fosters evolvement!

☯ Evolvement requires adaptability to change!

☯ The genius in how you predict and plan for change will determine your business future.

Expand "YOUR"
Vision...
Dare to be great!

- By removing myopia, possibilities come into view. Approach with an open mind!

- Willingness to consider and act upon possibilities opens the door to greatness!

- Just because you dare to be great, does not guarantee your desired result. Greatness requires tenacity in the pursuit of your vision!

DISCIPLINE 3

PLAN!

THE PATH TO GET
WHAT YOU WANT

One of the hardest things for most entrepreneurs to do is to sit down and write a plan! Their desire to see, taste and smell their vision often causes them to forego the planning process. Development and thought is required at this stage. Diving right in to implementation is a *BIG MISTAKE... this is gambling!*

Benjamin Franklin (one of the Founding Fathers of the United States) said it best... "An ounce of prevention is worth a pound of cure!" In the case of the entrepreneur, if a little advanced planning goes a long way... imagine the possibilities a thorough, well designed plan can bring. *The dividends are boundless!*

Planning your vision should not be a set it and forget it process. Your plan should be dynamic... evolving over time as you, the entrepreneur and the business evolves.

It should flow with ease from one milestone to the next en route to attaining your vision.

It should leverage the natural strengths, abilities and resources available to you, the entrepreneur.

The bottom line... the plan is not real unless it is written. That written expression of your plan is what we refer to as a *Managed Action Plan* or *MAP* for short! Your MAP can take on whatever physical form you, the entrepreneur deems appropriate.

PLANNING IN ADVANCE...
is a
SURE BET!

Clarify Your

Vision...

Plan with precision!

- Conceptualizing your vision initiates the planning process. You cannot plan what you cannot see!

- Rehearsing the vision in your minds-eye increases the likelihood of its successful attainment!

- Commit your vision to paper, enroll your team and take action!

insight 16

A Well Designed Plan
Becomes Alive...
Put it in writing!

- A Managed Action Plan (MAP) is the written expression of the vision. It documents the step-by-step process!

- Choose a format (e.g. spreadsheet, document, hand written, etc.) for your MAP that creates ease and efficiency for your team!

- Share your MAP using a medium (e.g. email, shared computer, cloud technology, etc.) that is readily accessible to all!

A Well Designed Plan Is
Modular...
Logically compartmentalized!

- Compartmentalizing allows for plug-and-play within your MAP thus allowing you to maximize resources and reduce potential for overwhelm!

- Every module has its own goals and objectives which in the end combine to meet your vision!

- Assign a "champion" for each module tasked with the responsibility of ensuring its success!

insight 18

A Well Designed Plan
Sails...
Captain your objectives!

- ❧ Fine tuning each module to maximize that which is in your control will increase the potential for achieving your desired result.

- ❧ The intention is to design your MAP so it flows effortlessly from module-to-module. Completion of each module fuels subsequent module(s).

- ❧ Assigning due dates, ownership, and accountability partners for each task within the modules ensures clarity, flow, and accomplishment.

A Well Designed Plan Is
Dynamic...
An "evolving" playbook!

- Unexpected events can and will happen. Even the best laid plans are rarely bulletproof. Anticipating where turbulence may occur is key!

- Dynamic plans incorporate a degree of flexibility. Without flexibility you are liable to break rather than bend. The intention is to be able to course correct as needed to get back on track as quickly and painlessly as possible!

- A dynamic plan incorporates predesigned alternate approaches!

insight 20

A Well Designed Plan Is
Risk Tolerant...
Leave no stone unturned!

- ☯ A risk tolerant plan accounts for and addresses the unexpected. It predetermines the course of action should a specific risk manifest (e.g. Accept the risk, Mitigate the risk, or Eliminate the risk)!

- ☯ Proper risk handling requires prioritization of identified risks based on its likelihood and anticipated impact!

- ☯ Effective risk taking is an educational process... it is not gambling or throwing caution to the wind... it is on purpose!

A Well Designed Plan
Reflects...

Mirror the desires, abilities, and energy of the team!

- ❧ Identify beyond the obvious characteristics of each of your team members for the purpose of leveraging their talents!

- ❧ Properly leveraging the distinct characteristics of each team member in relation to what the plan warrants, allows for maximization of human capital!

- ❧ Ongoing evaluation of team member characteristics is an ongoing process!

DISCIPLINE 4
LEAD !
INSPIRE TO ACHIEVE
EXCELLENCE

*H*aving a great vision for your business is not enough. Strong leadership is required to deliver that vision into reality. Doing so requires many skills and much discipline. Leadership is the glue that brings it all together so those involved, happily strive in unison toward the same big picture!

The effective leader is humble yet strong!

The effective leader seeks to inspire rather than motivate!

The effective leader acts as a beacon that light(s) the way for the team to follow!

The effective leader brings out the best in their team... it is quite common to see them draw extraordinary results out of seemingly ordinary people!

The effective leader seeks to serve rather than be served!

The effective leader acts as a unifier... bringing people together with ease!

The effective leader embraces risk and channels fear to act as a stimulant!

Yes, the effective leader is human and makes mistakes. The key is they take responsibility for the actions of both themselves and their team!

THE EFFECTIVE LEADER...
creates
SYNERGY
in the sandbox!

Contrarians Are

Visionaries...

Go where others fear to tread!

- ☯ Being contrarian should not be the driving force. Be contrarian only when it supports your vision!

- ☯ Visionaries dare to be great and push the limits beyond the commonly acceptable way!

- ☯ Visionaries act in spite of fear!

Lead By

Example...

Be willing to do whatever it takes!

- ☯ Leaders who walk their talk inspire others to follow intelligently!

- ☯ Leaders can anticipate the actual limits despite the limiting perceptions of others!

- ☯ The true leader demonstrates service above self!

Perception
Is Reality...
Know your true reflection!

- Authenticity requires knowing who you truly are and how others perceive you. That perception is the only truth!

- Gauging how you are truly showing up for others is key at all times. This is where trusted advisors are essential!

- Over time perceptions change... which means reality changes... which means new truths emerge... adaptation to change is essential!

insight 25

Contemplation is not
Procrastination...
Take decisive action!

- ☯ Taking the time to think things through is the sign of an educated mind!

- ☯ Employing left and right-brained thinking leads to more balanced resolutions!

- ☯ Learn to trust your instincts... often your first sense is the right one!

Delegate

or Stagnate...

Trust and show faith in your team!

- ☯ Articulate your vision in a manner that enables your team to engage effectively... They cannot deliver on what has not been clearly expressed!

- ☯ The effective leader knows when to intervene and to when to let go!

- ☯ Communicating specific actions as well as the desired result gives your team the opportunity to succeed!

insight 27

Push
the Right Buttons...
Inspiration goes further than motivation!

- ☯ The effective leader takes the time needed to truly understand what is important to each team member!

- ☯ The objective is to get your team to do what is needed because they want to!

- ☯ True inspiration eliminates the need for constant motivation!

Communicate
Your Vision...
Share the game plan not just the plays!

☯ Getting the team to appreciate the overall picture enables them to implement more purposefully!

☯ Individualizing communication based on the unique learning modality (e.g. visual, auditory, or kinesthetic) of each team member is needed to keep all on the same page!

☯ Much like a jigsaw puzzle, the effective leader communicates how the pieces (members) fit and support one another to accomplish the vision!

*W*hen it comes to communicating, the French proverb "plus ça change, plus c'est la même chose" really applies. The English translation... "the more that things change, the more they stay the same". Technological advances and mediums such as social media have not changed the rules of the game of communication. At its core, people are still people. They are driven by the same core desires they were centuries ago... to be loved... to be free... to have a purpose... and to be understood.

What technology has done is change the way the game of communication is played... empowering people to become more connected and social than ever before... a bit counterintuitive when one envisions people communicating while hiding behind their computer. However, technology has complicated the art of communicating in such that it masks the nuances of face-to-face communication such as tonality, intonation and physical expression.

Ironically, the world is seemingly shrinking. Access to one another has become simpler, more immediate, less expensive, and yet more complex.

The challenge when it comes to communication is remaining true to why you are communicating for your business in the first place and then leveraging technology effectively to enhance your efforts. Fruitful connections are not formed by happenstance. Throughout this resource you will see that having a plan is key.

Nothing happens in business without people. Communication is the vehicle that enables constructive interaction... regardless of media.

Communication should be precise, clear, and to the point. Every word should support the intention, purpose, and objective.

COMMUNICATION
is a
DANCE
...and so is the Tango!

Clarify

Purpose and Objective...

Apply it for optimal result!

- ☯ Effectively crafted communication inspires others and brings your "why" to life!

- ☯ Approach all engagements with a well-conceived game plan. Preparation opens possibility!

- ☯ Begin with the end in mind... focus on the desired result!

insight 30

Communicate
Clearly...

Deliver the essence of your intention!

- ☯ Words must be chosen with purpose. Eradicate hedge words. They weaken your message (i.e. 'try', 'sort of', 'kind of', etc.). Get to the point!

- ☯ Beware the 'ums' and 'ahs'. They convey uncertainty!

- ☯ Pace your words carefully so the intent of your message is properly received!

Listen

Intentionally...

Master this skill and watch your relationships and business soar!

❧ Listening is one skill that is not sufficiently taught in school. Mastery requires conscious awareness and self development!

❧ Two great rules to live by when engaging in conversation is... first, "listen twice and speak once" and second, "pause before speaking". These rules encourage conscious listening!

❧ Listening with the intention to understand is one of the greatest gifts you could give!

insight 32

Communicate
Intelligently...
Know how your message is translating!

- ☯ Be cognizant of whom you are speaking with. Take notice of body language, facial expressions and eye contact. They reveal receptivity!

- ☯ Trust your intuitive self. The energy you sense is most likely correct!

- ☯ Learn from every interaction. Positive actions are the proof that your message was accurately received!

People Have Dominant

Modalities...

Accommodate Them!

- ☯ The language one uses reveals their dominant learning modality (i.e. Visual, Auditory or Kinesthetic)!

- ☯ Pairing the proper learning modality to the audience is essential. People respond best when they are in their comfort zone!

- ☯ Use multiple forms of communication so that each learning modality is addressed!

insight 34

Technology
Rocks...
*Use as an enhancer (not a substitute)
for personal connection!*

- ☯ Your computer is not meant to be a mask. There is no substitute for in person connectivity. Proximity allows for experiencing energy!

- ☯ Tried and true methods such as hand-written notes are even more powerful in a technology laden world!

- ☯ Technology empowers you to connect more frequently and immediately regardless of where you are physically located!

Know

What They Want & Why...

Deeper understanding improves communicative effectiveness!

- ☯ Study your target market. Read what they read. Watch what they watch. Go where they go!

- ☯ Engage your target market. Spend time with them. Play what they play. Eat what they eat!

- ☯ Accept your target market without judgment. When you judge, you eliminate understanding!

DISCIPLINE 6
MARKET!
MAGNETIC ATTRACTION

*B*usinesses do not exist without clients. Clients do not know about a business without its marketing. Here is the rub... marketing is not dependent on huge sums of capital. Marketing is dependent on creativity and moxie.

The purpose for marketing is 3-fold...
1. Increase those who *'know'* you by expanding your *REACH* within your target market;
2. Increase those who *'like'* you by increasing your *VISIBILITY* with those who *know* you;
3. Increase those who *'trust'* you by building your CREDIBILITY with those who *know* and *like* you.

People do business with people they *know, like and trust...* it is that simple... and it is the responsibility of marketing to lay that groundwork. If done effectively, marketing gives birth to sales.

Effective marketing begins with clarity on whom you wish to serve... *your target market...* what you wish to serve them with... *your solutions...* and why... *your reason for being in business in the first place.*

It continues with the where, when and how you intend to establish and develop your relationship with your target market... *your marketing plan.*

And proceeds indefinitely with a commitment to strategically engage your target market in a manner they resonate with... remaining tastefully persistent unless asked to do otherwise.

SEEK ENGAGEMENT...
prior to
MARRIAGE!

Step Up Your

Marketing...

Great marketing paves the way for easier sales!

- ☯ Marketing creates the flow that feeds the sales pipeline thus resulting in business growth!

- ☯ Employ marketing strategies with specific objectives in mind and measurements to gauge!

- ☯ Less is more... seek to increase the effectiveness of each marketing touch!

insight 37

Aim for the
Heart...
Choose the precise target!

- ☯ When choosing your ideal target market, ensure they are hungry for what you offer... can afford your offering... are easily reachable... there are enough of them around... and you like them!

- ☯ The more targeted your marketing, the more responsive your audience becomes... the more responsive your audience becomes, the more sales!

- ☯ Further segmenting your target market by demographic, geographic and psychographic data will significantly increase the effectiveness of your marketing!

Beware the

Siren Song...

Employ marketing tools and platforms that make sense!

- ☯ Businesses are regularly bombarded with pressure to use presumably 'hot' marketing tools and platforms... distinguish between reality and hype!

- ☯ Knowing how your target market prefers to be communicated with will help you determine your best marketing options!

- ☯ Your ideal blend of marketing tools and platforms should allow you to showcase your skills and style while remaining respectful to your budget.

insight 39

Market

Strategically...

*Move prospects systematically
toward your objective!*

☯ Train your prospects to follow your lead by
providing a clear path that is painless,
profitable, and pleasurable for them to
follow and benefit from!

☯ Present a clear call-to-action on each
marketing piece and reward prospects
when they follow through!

☯ Strategic marketing campaigns are
carefully coordinated to ensure top-of-
mind awareness without being invasive!

insight 40

Diversify
Or Die...
Mitigate your marketing risk!

- Having multiple marketing tactics and strategies operating across more than one medium reduces risk and expands your chances of fulfilling your sales objectives.

- Successful businesses tend to each have a unique recipe for their marketing... develop your own recipe!

- Have a contingency plan for your marketing... if one strategy or tactic underperforms or fails; be ready to pick up the slack with another!

insight 41

Command
Attention...
Be bold and compelling from the outset!

ꙮ Most people innately want to be led and effective marketing and marketers are up for the opportunity!

ꙮ Marketing that leads with attention grabbing headlines and/or powerful imagery significantly improves its chances of standing out amongst a sea of distraction!

ꙮ Dare to be creatively different!

Be Loving and
Lovable...
To those you wish to serve!

- ❦ Effective marketing elicits emotion and is not afraid to polarize those not in its ideal target!

- ❦ Engage your ideal target market in a way that makes them feel heard, understood, and special!

- ❦ Relationships do require work; however, love is the strongest bond two people can share. Love encourages loyalty!

*T*he great salesperson understands that people buy according to their own processing cycle and are willing to allow it to run its course.

Imposing your will on a prospect does not create goodwill... it can create a purchaser; however, until they willingly enter the buying process you are facing resistance. The sales process should not be a tug-of-war.

Mutually beneficial sales result in a win/win. The buyer receives what is in their best interest and the salesperson accomplishes their professional objective as well as a feeling that money cannot buy... we call this the "Mitzvah Exchange".

Business is the backbone to a healthy economy.

Sales stimulate that backbone, increasing the flow and thus keeping the economy strong.

Consumer confidence is driven more by the perception of the economy than the actual state at hand. Therefore, your ability to increase consumer confidence by offering viable solutions to real-world challenges is paramount to the health of the economy.

'Sales' is a positive. It is necessary. Embrace the process of sales!

JOY TO THE WORLD...
SALES
are made!

Develop

Clients...

Eliminate desire to look elsewhere!

- ☯ Clients see relationship with the provider as indispensible!

- ☯ Customers see sales offerings as commodities... loyalty has not been developed!

- ☯ Intentional language impacts how you will be considered as a provider. Interpretation of that language will determine the development of a client or a customer!

insight 44

Emotions
Drive Sales...
Uncover what's important!

- ☯ Appealing to logic does not drive sales; it supports them after the fact!

- ☯ Intentional language needs to trigger an emotion that causes the desired action!

- ☯ Knowledge of human behavior and the desires of your target market are essential for a successful sales campaign!

Emphasize

Value...

The strongest way to compete!

☯ When you compete on price alone, you and your competition lose... potentially driving each other out of business!

☯ You cannot survive in business for long by being a price-driven commodity. There will always be a competitor willing to charge less than you!

☯ Providing value maintains long term relationships!

insight 46

Walk

Your Talk...

Your USP must be your SOP!

๑ It is all about dharma (look it up)... it is your obligation to stay true to your word!

๑ Your USP (Unique Selling Position) is your attempt to influence your target market on how you want them to see you and why. It is the essence of what you want your brand to be.

๑ Your SOP (Standard Operating Procedure) is the act of performing your USP!

insight 47

You
Are In Sales...
There is no business without sales!

☯ Sales is honorable... respect it!

☯ Create a methodology for generating sales... the better your systems and procedures, the more good you can deliver!

☯ The sales engine should never idle... ongoing and strategic sales activity is the fuel for successful results!

insight 48

Deliver

Solutions...

The purpose of your offering!

- ☯ Clients are buying solutions and that is what they deserve!

- ☯ Design or construct your offering with results in mind!

- ☯ Allowing for feedback is an effective way to uncover other challenges to be solved!

Absorb

Risk...

Allow sales to flow!

- Risk is emotional and it's that emotion that makes or breaks a sale!

- Your belief in your offering and willingness to stand behind it instills confidence removing uncertainty from the buyer!

- Uncertainty leads to the emotional state of confusion and a confused mind does not buy!

*T*o assist you in getting the most out of this book, the diagram that follows is a system that we call the "Power of SEVEN". SEVEN is an acronym for:

- ☯ Stretch *your mind...*
- ☯ Establish *objective...*
- ☯ Visualize *results...*
- ☯ Empower *manifestation...*
- ☯ Nurture *growth...*

Running this system against any or all of the insights provided in this book will help you draw the most value out of each one. Working on these insights with a mentor, coach, and or mastermind group is suggested.

The Power of SEVEN

Stretch *your mind...*
Based on the insight, what is your "aha"?

Establish *objective...*
Based on the insight, what will you commit to? Why?

Visualize *results...*
Based on the insight, what are you seeing as your objective is realized?

Empower *manifestation...*
Based on the insight, what one (1) action are you willing to take right now toward realizing your objective?

Nurture *growth...*
Based on the insight, what are you committed to doing on an ongoing basis?

Stretch *Your Mind!*

Action Step...
Based on the insight, what is your "aha"?

Coaching Moment...
Reach deep into your inner child. Fantasize and imagine your world if failure was neither an option... nor even a thought.

Edification...
An "aha" moment is when the light bulb goes on and you feel like you have had a breakthrough in your thinking.

_____

_____

_____

_____

_____

_____

_____

_____

_____

Establish *Objective!*

Action Step...
Based on the insight, what will you commit to? Why?

Coaching Moment...
Distinguish between 'Busyness' versus 'Business'.

Focus...
Does your commitment accomplish your intention?

Edification...
'Busyness' is not solution oriented, 'Business' is.

_____

_____

_____

_____

_____

_____

_____

_____

Visualize *Results!*

Action Step...
Based on the insight, what are you seeing as your objective is realized?

Coaching Moment...
Fantasize and imagine that your objective has been realized. Be in that moment.

Edification...
The insights in Discipline 1 'Believe' are required to visualize results.

_____

_____

_____

_____

_____

_____

_____

_____

_____

Empower *Manifestation!*

Action Step...

Based on the insight, what one (1) action are you willing to take right now toward realizing your objective?

Coaching Moment...

The manifestation of your objective requires you being in action. Fantasizing and visualizing is not enough.

Edification...

Actions need to be in the right order, directed at the right purpose, in order to manifest your objective.

_____

_____

_____

_____

_____

_____

_____

_____

Nurture *Growth!*

Action Step...
Based on the insight, what are you committed to doing on an ongoing basis?

Coaching Moment...
Continuously focused and purposeful action is the key to nurturing growth. Being okay with realized growth is critical to sustaining your success.

Edification...
All growth requires being okay with some degree of risk. Be comfortable with being uncomfortable.

Postscript

In this resource, we have provided you with a guide to propel you further along your path to achieving your dreams.

Achieving objectives is a start. Functioning like this on a daily basis is your charge.

EVOLVE
to
ACTUALIZATION!

No matter where you are on your journey, traveling alone is rarely the best option.

The Mindstretch Mastermind
Get together with fellow entrepreneurs to work through the insights!

The Mindstretch Coaching
Work 1-on-1 or in a group setting with a Mindstretch professional to mentor you!

The Mindstretch Workshop Series
Live programs meant to go deeper with the insights!
(customizable for organizations)

Visit www.TheMindstretch.com to learn more!

Dean Mercado, President of Online Marketing Muscle®
is a well-respected marketing coach, strategist, author,
and speaker with expertise on helping businesses and
independent professionals increase their visibility,
credibility, and reach within their target market.

Barry Laub, President of Infinite Resources, Inc. is a
highly sought after business visionary, strategist,
author and entertaining motivational speaker. Barry is
known for taking businesses and individuals from
where they are to where they want to be.

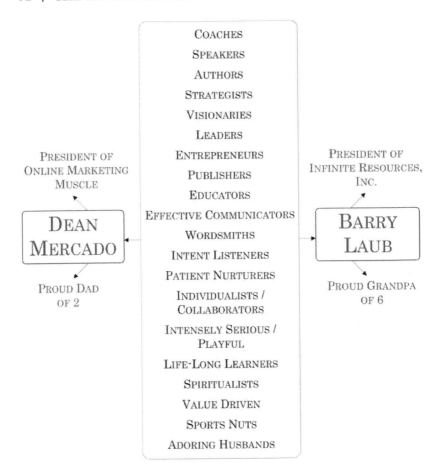

COACHES

SPEAKERS

AUTHORS

STRATEGISTS

VISIONARIES

LEADERS

ENTREPRENEURS

PUBLISHERS

EDUCATORS

EFFECTIVE COMMUNICATORS

WORDSMITHS

INTENT LISTENERS

PATIENT NURTURERS

INDIVIDUALISTS / COLLABORATORS

INTENSELY SERIOUS / PLAYFUL

LIFE-LONG LEARNERS

SPIRITUALISTS

VALUE DRIVEN

SPORTS NUTS

ADORING HUSBANDS

PRESIDENT OF ONLINE MARKETING MUSCLE

DEAN MERCADO

PROUD DAD OF 2

PRESIDENT OF INFINITE RESOURCES, INC.

BARRY LAUB

PROUD GRANDPA OF 6

Made in the USA
Lexington, KY
19 July 2013